ONE HUNDRED
Kisses

ALSO BY CELIA HADDON

One Hundred Ways to Say Thank You

One Hundred Ways to Be Happy

One Hundred Ways to Say I Love You

One Hundred Ways to Friendship

One Hundred Ways to Serenity

One Hundred Ways to a Happy Cat

One Hundred Ways to a Happy Dog

One Hundred Ways for a
Cat to Train Its Human

One Hundred Ways for a
Cat to Find Its Inner Kitten

One Hundred Secret Thoughts
Cats have about Humans

ONE HUNDRED
Kisses

BY

Celia Haddon

Hodder & Stoughton
LONDON SYDNEY AUCKLAND

British Library Cataloguing in Publication Data
A record for this book is available from
the British Library

ISBN 0 340 90863 7

Printed and bound in Great Britain
by Bookmarque Ltd,
Croydon, Surrey

The paper and board used in this paperback are natural
recyclable products made from wood grown in sustainable
forests. The manufacturing processes conform to the
environmental regulations of the country of origin.

Hodder & Stoughton
A Division of Hodder Headline Ltd
338 Euston Road
London NW1 3BH
www.madaboutbooks.com

To Ronnie.... Kisses, kisses, kisses.

Contents

Definitions, Descriptions and Declarations

A kiss is something you cannot give without taking and cannot take without giving.

ANONYMOUS

A kiss without a hug is like a flower without the fragrance.

MALTESE PROVERB

Come hither womankind and all their
     worth,
  Give me thy kisses as I call them forth.
Give me the billing kiss, that of the dove,
  A kiss of love;
The melting kiss, a kiss that doth
     consume
  To a perfume;
The extract kiss, of every sweet a part,
  A kiss of art;
The kiss which ever stirs some new
     delight,
  A kiss of might;
The twaching smacking kiss, and
     when you cease,
  A kiss of peace;

The music kiss, crochet-and-quaver time;
  The kiss of rhyme;
The kiss of eloquence, which doth
   belong
  Unto the tongue;
The kiss of all the sciences in one,
  The Kiss alone.

EDWARD, LORD HERBERT OF
CHERBURY,
poet, 1583–1648

K isses that are easily obtained
are easily forgotten.

ENGLISH PROVERB

K isses don't last; cookery do.

GEORGE MEREDITH,
novelist, 1828–1909

Y ou have to kiss a lot of frogs,
before you meet your prince.

PROVERB

There is the kiss of welcome and of parting, the long, lingering, loving, present one; the stolen, or the mutual one; the kiss of love, of joy, and of sorrow; the seal of promise and receipt of fulfilment.

THOMAS C. HALIBURTON,
judge and author, 1796–1865

The sound of a kiss is not so loud as that of a cannon, but its echo lasts a great deal longer.

OLIVER WENDELL HOLMES,
essayist and poet, 1809–94

Are kisses all? – they but forerun
  Another duty to be done:
What would you of that minstrel say,
  Who tunes his pipe, and will not play?
Say, what are blossoms in their prime
  That ripen not in harvest time?
O what are buds that ne'er disclose
  The longed-for sweetness of the rose?
So kisses to a lover's guest
  Are invitations, not the feast.

THOMAS RANDOLPH,
poet and playwright, 1605–35

Kissing is nature's way of helping to keep teeth clean. When people kiss, it stimulates the flow of saliva. And the saliva helps wash away the sugar solutions that cause plaque on the teeth. Chewing gum does the same thing but kissing is more fun.

BARRY KEEN,
dentist, living

Among thy fancies, tell me this,
  What is the thing we call a kiss?...
It is a creature born and bred
  Between the lips, all cherry red,
By love and warm desires fed.

ROBERT HERRICK,
poet and clergyman, 1591–1674

A kiss on the hand means 'I adore you.' A kiss on the cheek means 'I just want to be friends.' A kiss on the neck means 'I want you.' A kiss on the lips means 'I love you.'

FOLKLORE

A man may drink and no be drunk;
A man may fight and no be slain;
A man may kiss a bonnie lass,
And aye be welcome back again.

ROBERT BURNS,
poet, 1759–96

Many mammals 'kiss' before mating as a way of stimulating a partner's maternal instincts. Dolphins nibble, cats give playful bites, dogs lick faces or nuzzle flanks, and chimps press lips in their courtship. Our kiss originates from a mammal-wide sucking reflex.

DAVID GIVENS,
anthropologist, living

The First Kiss

Every marriage, every love affair, and every unhappy passion begins with the first kiss. It is the gateway to passionate love or passionate hate, to heaven or hell. The first kiss has within it the possibilities of glorious consummation, the full flowering of a lifetime love, the bitterness of final betrayal or the despair of loss.

AUTHOR UNKNOWN

'Twas a new feeling – something
   more
  Than we had dared to own before,
Which then we hid not;
  We saw it in each other's eye,
And wished in every broken sigh
  To speak, but did not!

She felt my lips' impassioned touch;
  'Twas the first time I dared so
    much,
And yet she chid not;
  But whispered o'er my burning
    brow,
'Oh! do you doubt I love you now?'
  Sweet soul! I did not.

THOMAS MOORE,
poet, 1779–1852

Women still remember the first kiss after men have forgotten the last.

REMY DE GOURMONT,
novelist, 1858–1915

First time he kissed me, he but only
    kissed
The fingers of this hand wherewith I
    write;
And ever since, it grew o'er clean
    and white,
Slow to world-greetings, quick with
    its 'Oh, list,'
When the angels speak. A ring of
    amethyst
I could not wear here, plainer to my
    sight
Than that first kiss.

ELIZABETH BARRETT BROWNING,
poet, 1806–61

With what language shall I address my lovely fair to acquaint her with the sentiments of a heart she delights to torture? I have not a minute's quiet out of your sight; and when I am with you, you use me with so much distance, that I am still in a state of absence, heightened with a view of the charms which I am denied to approach. In a word, you must give me either a fan, a mask, or a glove you have worn, or I cannot live; otherwise you must expect that I'll kiss your hand, or, when I next sit by you, steal your handkerchief.

RICHARD STEELE,
writer, to his future wife, 1707

It takes a lot of experience for a girl to kiss like a beginner.

AUTHOR UNKNOWN

Ah, I remember well – and how
    can I
But ever more remember well –
    when first
Our flame began ...
Then would we kiss, then sigh, then
    look: and thus
In that first garden of our simpleness
We spent our childhood ...

SAMUEL DANIEL,
poet, 1562–1619

So sweet love seemed that April
  morn,
  When first we kissed beside the
  thorn,
So strangely sweet, it was not strange
  We thought that love could never
  change.

But I can tell – let truth be told –
  That love will change in growing
  old!
Though day to day is nought to see
  So delicate his motions be.

ROBERT BRIDGES,
poet, 1844–1930

May his soul be in heaven – he deserves it, I'm sure – who was first the inventor of kissing.

ANONYMOUS

'I saw you take his kiss!' ''Tis true.'
'O, modesty!' ''Twas strictly kept:
He thought me asleep; at least I
  knew
  He thought I thought he thought I
  slept.'

      COVENTRY PATMORE,
      poet, 1823–96

It has been said by them of old time, and our fathers have told us, that the kiss of first love, the first kiss of the first woman we love, is beyond all kisses sweet; and true it is. But true is it also that no less sweet is the first kiss of the last woman we love.

RICHARD LE GALLIENNE,
writer, 1866–1947

When age chills the blood, when our
  pleasures are past –
 For years flee away with the wings
  of the dove –
The dearest remembrance will still
  be the last,
 Our sweetest memorial the first kiss
  of love.

LORD GEORGE BYRON,
poet, 1788–1824

Truly, Helen, my dearest and most beloved, I found the splendour of yesterday's joy almost frightening. I have kissed you! I had to join my lips with yours, I was driven irresistibly, by some inner force I would not escape. So much ecstasy all at once, my eyes were wet with tears, all my body and soul swamped in one great flood of emotion. This is how much I love you.

Dazed with delight, I staggered homewards, feeling only your sweet hand caressing my soul. I was rocked in bliss, bearing home on my lips the most glorious of kisses.

ALBAN BERG,
composer, to his future wife, 1907

Asking, Begging and Demanding

For love's sake kiss me once again;
  I long, and should not beg in vain –
Here's none to spy or see;
  Why do you doubt or stay?
I'll taste as lightly as the bee
  That doth but touch his flower, and
  flies away.

BEN JONSON,
playwright and poet, 1572–1637

In short, my deary! Kiss me and be quiet.

LADY MARY WORTLEY MONTAGU,
writer, 1689–1762

And if you'll blow to me a kiss
I'll blow a kiss to you.

JAMES SMITH,
comic poet, 1775–1839

Kiss, lovely Celia, and be kind:
Let my desires freedom find,
  Sit thee down,
And we will make the gods confess
Mortals enjoy some happiness …

> THOMAS CAREW,
> poet, 1595–1639

L et him kiss me with the kisses
of his mouth: for thy love is
better than wine.

THE SONG OF SONGS, I:2, KJV

This dog may kiss your hand,
   your lip,
 Lie in your lap, and with you
   sleep,
On the same pillow rest his head,
 Be your companion in your
   bed.
Now he that gave it doth not
   crave
 Any reward of what he gave;
But he would think himself more
   blest
 If you'd but use him as a beast.

     ANONYMOUS,
    seventeenth century

Drink to me with thine eyes only; or, if thou wilt, putting the cup to thy lips, fill it with kisses, and so bestow it upon me. I, as soon as I behold thee, thirst; and, taking hold of the cup, do not indeed apply that to my lips but thee.

FLAVIUS PHILOSTRATUS,
orator and author, c.170– c.244

Was this the face that launched a
    thousand ships,
And burnt the topless towers of
    Ilium?
Sweet Helen, make me immortal
    with a kiss!
Her lips suck forth my soul; see
    where it flies!
Come, Helen, come, give me my
    soul again.
Here will I dwell, for heaven is in
    those lips,
And all is dross that is not Helena.

CHRISTOPHER MARLOW,
playwright and poet, 1664–93

What is love? 'tis not hereafter;
  Present mirth hath present laughter;
What's to come is still unsure:
  In delay there lies no plenty;
Then come kiss me, sweet-and-
    twenty,
  Youth's a stuff will not endure.

WILLIAM SHAKESPEARE,
playwright, 1564–1616

Kiss Me Quick.

TRADITIONAL SEASIDE MOTTO

The bee's kiss, now!
Kiss me as if you entered gay
My heart at some noonday,
A bud that dares not disallow
The claim, so all is rendered up,
And passively its shattered cup
Over your head to sleep I bow.

ROBERT BROWNING,
poet, 1812–89

See the mountains kiss high heaven
And the waves clasp one another;
No sister-flower would be forgiven
If it disdained its brother,
And the sunlight clasps the earth
And the moonbeams kiss the sea:
What is all this sweet work worth
If thou kiss not me?

PERCY BYSSHE SHELLEY,
poet, 1792–1822

Romantic Kisses

Her kisses are
Soft as a snow-tuft in the dewless cup
Of a redoubled rose, noiselessly
    falling
When heaven is brimful of starry
    night.

THOMAS LOVELL BEDDOES,
poet and doctor, 1803–49

Their lips drew near, and clung into
    a kiss;
A long, long kiss, a kiss of youth, and
    love,
And beauty, all concentrating like
    rays
Into one focus, kindled them above;
Such kisses as belong to early days,
Where heart, and soul, and sense in
    concert move,
And the blood's lava, and the pulse a
    blaze,
Each kiss a heart-quake – for a kiss's
    strength,
I think, it must be reckoned by its
    length.

LORD GEORGE BYRON,
poet, 1788–1824

Whom I best loved, alone I met
  unmanned.
 I kissed her: thus far manners did
  command.
But when I had her sweet lips once
  but tasted
 I thought all time not spent in
  kissing wasted.
Manners farewell! I needs must
  farther go.
 'We private are now, sweet, say me
  not no.'

AUTHOR UNKNOWN,
seventeenth century

Without understanding anything of this mystery I kissed this charming friend … But what happened to me a moment later when I felt … my hand shakes … a sweet trembling … your rosy lips … Julia's lips … placed, pressed on mine, and my body clasped in your arms! No, the lightning from heaven is not keener or more sudden than that which came then to consume me. All my senses thrilled at that delicious touch, and my heart died under the pain of that pleasure … I scarcely know what has happened to me from that fatal moment. The profound impression I received can never be effaced.

JEAN-JACQUES ROUSSEAU,
philosopher, 1712–78

Jenny kissed me when we met,
  Jumping from the chair she sat in.
Time, you thief, who love to get
  Sweets into your list, put that in.
Say I'm weary, say I'm sad;
  Say that health and wealth have
    missed me;
Say I'm growing old, but add –
  Jenny kissed me!

LEIGH HUNT
1784–1859

O that joy so soon should waste!
　Or so sweet a bliss
　　As a kiss
Might not for ever last!
　So sugared, so melting, so soft,
　　so delicious,
　　　The dew that lies on roses,
　　　When the morn itself discloses,
　　　　Is not so precious.
O rather than I would it smother,
　Were I to taste such another,
　　It should be my wishing
　　That I might die kissing.

BEN JONSON,
playwright and poet, 1572–1637

My Darling whispered Bernard and he seiezed her in his arms we will be marrid next week.

Oh Bernard muttered Ethel this is so sudden.

No no cried Bernard and taking the bull by both horns he kissed her violently on her dainty face. My bride to be he murmered several times.

Ethel trembled with joy as she heard the mystick words.

Oh Bernard she said little did I ever dream of such as this and she suddenly fainted into his out stretched arms.

DAISY ASHFORD,
written when aged nine,
1881–1972

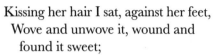

Kissing her hair I sat, against her feet,
  Wove and unwove it, wound and
    found it sweet;
Made fast therewith her hands, drew
    down her eyes,
  Deep as deep flowers and dreamy
    like dim skies;

With her own tresses bound and
found her fair,
Kissing her hair.

ALGERNON SWINBURNE,
poet, 1837–1909

Hey, the dusty miller
And his dusty coat!
He will spend a shilling
Or he will win a groat.
Dusty was the coat,
Dusty was the colour,
Dusty was the kiss
That I gat frae the miller!

ROBERT BURNS,
poet, 1759–96

Not believe that I love you?...
Recall to mind what happened last night. That at least was a lover's kiss. Its eagerness, its fierceness, its warmth, expressed the god its parent. But oh! its sweetness, and its melting softness, expressed him more. With trembling in my limbs, and fevers in my soul I ravish'd it. Convulsions, pantings, murmurings shew'd the mighty disorder within me; the mighty disorder increased by it. For those dear lips shot through my heart, and through my bleeding vitals, delicious poison, and an avoidless but yet charming ruin.

WILLIAM CONGREVE
to Mrs Arabella Hunt, 1690

I felt the while a pleasing kind of
    smart,
The kiss went tingling to my
    panting heart:
When it was gone, the sense of it
    did stay,
The sweetness cling'd upon my lips
    all day,
Like drops of honey, loath to fall
    away.

JOHN DRYDEN,
poet and playwright, 1631–1700

My sweet did sweetly sleep,
And on her rosy face
Stood tears of pearl, which beauty's
    self did weep;
I, wondering at her grace,
Did all amazed remain,
When Love said, 'Fool, can looks thy
    wishes crown?
Time past comes not again.'
Then did I me bow down,
And kissing her fair breast, lips,
    cheeks, and eyes,
Proved here on earth the joys of
    paradise.

WILLIAM DRUMMOND OF
    HAWTHORNDEN,
    poet, 1585–1649

Platonic Kisses

I dare not ask a kiss;
  I dare not beg a smile,
Lest having that, or this,
  I might grow proud the while.

No, no, the utmost share
  Of my desire shall be
Only to kiss that air
  That lately kissed thee.

ROBERT HERRICK,
poet and clergyman, 1591–1674

Next came the Queen (Elizabeth 1), in the sixty-fifth year of her age, as we are told, very majestic … Whoever speaks to her, it is kneeling; now and then she raises some with her hand. While we were there, W.

Slawata, a Bohemian baron, had letters to present to her; and she, after pulling off her glove, gave him her right hand to kiss, sparkling with rings and jewels, as a mark of particular favour. Wherever she turned her face everybody fell on their knees.

PAUL HENTZNER,
a visitor to the English court, 1598

K iss me, Hardy.

HORATIO NELSON,
admiral, on his deathbed, 1805

Little Lamb,
Here I am:
Come and lick
My white neck;
Let me pull
Your soft wool;
Let me kiss
Your soft face;
Merrily, merrily, we
    welcome in the year.

WILLIAM BLAKE,
artist and poet, 1757–1827

Golden slumbers kiss your eyes;
  Smiles awake you when you rise,
Sleep, pretty wantons, do not cry,
  And I will sing a lullaby.
Rock them, rock them, lullaby.

THOMAS DEKKER,
playwright and poet,
c.1570–1641

It is reported of Magdalen, Queen of France, and wife to Louis XI, a Scottish woman by birth, that walking forth in an evening with her ladies, she spied M. Alanus, one of the king's chaplains, a silly, old, hard-favoured man, fast asleep in a bower, and kissed him sweetly; when the young ladies laughed at her for it, she replied that it was not his person that she did embrace and reverence, but, with a platonic love, the divine beauty of his soul.

ROBERT BURTON,
psychologist and scholar, 1577–1640

The kiss of the sun for pardon,
  The song of the birds for mirth,
One is nearer God's heart in a
    garden,
  Than anywhere else on earth.

DOROTHY FRANCES GURNEY,
    poet, 1858–1932

For the very old, a kiss is an astonishment and a comfort.

PAM BROWN,
writer, living

Who ran to help me when I fell,
And would some pretty story tell,
Or kiss the place to make it well?
My mother.

ANN TAYLOR,
poet, 1782–1866

Forgiveness is the kiss of God.

PROVERB

Absence and Longing

By absence this good means I gain,
  That I can catch her,
Where none can watch her,
  In some close corner of my brain:
There I embrace and kiss her,
  And so I both enjoy and miss her.

JOHN HOSKINS,
poet, 1566–1638

My waking thoughts are all of thee ... My soul is broken with grief and there is no rest for your love. But is there more for me when, delivering ourselves up to the deep feelings which master me, I breathe out upon your lips, upon your heart, a flame which burns me up – ah, it was this past night I realised that your portrait was not you. You start at noon; I shall see you in three hours. Meanwhile, *mio dolce amor*, accept a thousand kisses, but give me none, for they fire my blood.

NAPOLEON BONAPARTE
to Josephine Beauharnais, 1796

No more to you at this present, mine own darling, for lack of time. But I would that you were in my arms, or I in yours – for I think it long since I kissed you. Written after the killing of a hart, at eleven of the clock; purposing with God's grace, tomorrow, mighty timely, to kill another, by the hand which, I trust, shortly shall be yours.

HENRY VIII
to Anne Boleyn, 1528

I wish my dear that you were here,
  And not so far away;
I'm sending you a good big kiss
  With all my love today.

FIRST WORLD WAR POSTCARD

My own dear Emma, I kiss the hands with all humbleness and gratitude, which have so filled up for me the cup of happiness – It is my most earnest wish I may make myself worthy of you.

CHARLES DARWIN
to his future wife, 1838

Oh that thou wert as my brother, that sucked the breasts of my mother! When I should find thee without, I would kiss thee; yea, I should not be despised.

THE SONG OF SONGS 8:1 KJV

I saw her crop a rose
Right early in the day,
And I went to kiss the place
Where the rose she broke away.

JOHN CLARE,
gardener and poet, 1793–1864

Goody, Goody, Dear Goody,

You said you would weary: and I do
hope in my heart you are wearying:
It will be so sweet to make it all up to
you in kisses when I return. You will
'*take me*' and hear all my bits of ex-
periences, and your heart will beat
faster when you find how I have
longed to return to you, Darling –

Dearest – Loveliest. 'The Lord bless you.' I think of you every hour, every moment, I love you and admire you like – like anything ...'

JANE CARLYLE,
to Thomas Carlyle, 1828

Might I but kiss thy hand! I dare
   not fold
My arms about thee – scarcely
   dare to speak.

And nothing seems to me so wild
    and bold,
As with one kiss to touch thy
    blessèd cheek.
Methinks if I should kiss thee, no
    control
Within the thrilling brain could
    keep afloat
The subtle spirit. Even while I
    spoke,
The bare word KISS hath made
    my inner soul
To tremble like a lutestring, ere
    the note
Hath melted in the silence that it
    broke.

ALFRED LORD TENNYSON,
poet, 1809–92

Strephon kissed me in the spring,
 Robin in the fall,
But Colin only looked at me
 And never kissed at all.

Strephon's kiss was lost in jest,
 Robin's lost in play,
But the kiss in Colin's eyes
 Haunts me night and day.

SARA TEASDALE,
poet, 1884–1933

I want to send back to my Aimee her little piece of paper with a hundred kisses on it, in order to beg her to place her lips on it again and to send it back to me anew. I have to admit that it smells of tobacco and the wax used on moustaches – when I saw it I did not think of making my mouth worthy of that mouth it represents. Not knowing the exact spot where you had touched it, I put my lips all over it – I would have devoured it had it been less precious …

ALFRED DE MUSSET
to Aimee D'Alton, April 1837

Fain would I kiss my Julia's dainty
 leg,
Which is as white and hairless as
 an egg.

ROBERT HERRICK,
poet and clergyman, 1591–1674

Disapproval, Disgust and Rejection

If your lover's had her face lifted
  You may find her lips have shifted.
If she's Botoxed and can't smile
  Kissing her may taste quite vile.
And if she's got a trout pout
  Kissing is out.

> JESS MCAREE,
> journalist, living

What lies lurk in kisses.

HEINRICH HEINE,
poet and essayist, 1797–1856

And the best and the worst of this is
  That neither is most to blame,
If you've forgotten my kisses,
  And I've forgotten your name.

ALGERNON SWINBURNE,
poet, 1837–1909

You are coming to woo me, but not
  as of yore,
  When I hastened to welcome your
  ring at the door;
For I trusted that he who stood
  waiting me then,
  Was the brightest, the truest, the
  noblest of men.
Your lips on my own when they
  printed 'Farewell,'
  Had never been soiled by the
  beverage of hell;
But they come to me now with the
  bacchanal sign,
  And the lips that touch liquor
  must never touch mine.

GEORGE W. YOUNG,
temperance writer, dates unknown

Faithful are the wounds of a friend: But the kisses of an enemy are deceitful.

PROVERBS 27:6, KJV

But had I wist, before I kissed,
 That love had been sae ill to win,
I had locked my heart in a case
    o'gowd,
  And pinn'd it with a siller pin.

SCOTTISH BALLAD

Ask me not, Phyllis, why I do refuse
  To kiss thee as the most of gallants
    use:
For seeing oft thy dog to fawn and
    skip
  Upon thy lap, and joining lip to lip,
Although thy kisses I full fain would
    crave,
  Yet would I not thy dog my rival
    have.

ANONYMOUS,
seventeenth century

See but how the form of salutations, which is peculiar to our nation (France), doth by its facility bastardize the grace of kisses … It is an unpleasing and injurious custom unto ladies, that they must afford their lips to any man that hath but three lackeys (servants) following him, how unhandsome and loathsome, soever he be. Nor do we ourselves gain much by it: for as the world is divided into four parts, so for four fair ones we must kiss fifty foul ….

MICHEL MONTAIGNE,
essayist, 1533–92

I abhor the slimey kiss,
  Which to me most loathsome is.
Those lips please me which are
    placed
  Close, but not too strictly laced:
Yielding I would have them; yet
  Not a wimbling tongue admit.

ROBERT HERRICK,
poet and clergyman, 1591–1674

Some people kiss and tell. Others kiss and don't tell. A few don't kiss but tell as if they did.

AUTHOR UNKNOWN

All night upon my heart I felt her
    warm heart beat,
Night-long within mine arms in love
    and sleep she lay;
Surely the kisses of her bought red
    mouth were sweet;
  But I was desolate and sick of an
    old passion,

When I awoke and found the dawn
   was grey:
I have been faithful to thee,
   Cynara! In my fashion.

ERNEST DOWSON,
poet, 1867–1900

Lord, I wonder what fool it was
first invented kissing.

JONATHON SWIFT,
satirist, 1667–1745

Sing jigmijole the pudding bowl,
The table and the frame,
My master he did cudgel me
For kissing of my dame.

The hunt is up,
The hunt is up,
And now it is almost day;
And he that's in bed with another
    man's wife,
It's time to get him away.

NURSERY RHYME

I did but crave that I might kiss,
  If not her lip, at least her hand,
The coolest lover's frequent bliss;
  And rude is she that will withstand
That inoffensive liberty:
  She (would you think it?) in a fume
Turned her about and left the room;
  Not she, she vowed, not she.

THOMAS FLATMAN,
painter and poet, 1635–67

Farewell Kisses

Since there's no help, come let us kiss
    and part;
Nay, I have done, you get no more of
    me,
And I am glad, yea, glad with all my
    heart
That thus so cleanly I myself can
    free.
Shake hands for ever, cancel all our
    vows,
And, when we meet at any time
    again,
Be it not seen in either of our brows
That we one jot of former love
    retain.

Now at the last gasp of Love's latest
    breath,
When, his pulse failing, Passion
    speechless lies,
When Faith is kneeling by his bed of
    death,
And Innocence is closing up his
    eyes,
  Now if thou wouldst, when all have
    given him over,
  From death to life, thou might'st
    him yet recover.

MICHAEL DRAYTON,
    poet, 1563–1631

A farewell kiss can be a talisman against all harm; a charm to hold a heart in gentle thrall; a thread to link our lives in spite of time and distance.

PAMELA DUGDALE,
writer, living

Take, take away thy smiles and
   kisses!
 Thy love wounds deeper than
   disdain,
For he that sees the heaven he misses
 Sustains two hells, of loss and pain …

THOMAS STANLEY,
lawyer and poet, 1625–78

That farewell kiss which re-
sembles greeting, that last
glance of love, which becomes
the sharpest pang of sorrow.

GEORGE ELIOT,
novelist, 1819–80

So, so break off this last lamenting kiss,
Which sucks two souls and vapours
   both away,
Turn you, ghost, that way, and let me
   turn this,
And let ourselves benight our happiest
   day.
We asked none leave to love; nor will
  we owe
Any, so cheap a death, as saying 'Go.'

JOHN DONNE,
poet and clergyman, 1572–1631

On a time the amorous Silvy
Said to her shepherd, 'Sweet, how do
   you?

Kiss me this once, and then God be wi'
    you,
                My sweetest dear!
Kiss me this once and then God be wi'
    you,
For now the morning draweth near.' ...

With that the shepherd waked from
    sleeping,
And, spying where the day was
    peeping,
He said, 'Now take my soul in keeping,
                My sweetest dear!
Kiss me, and take my soul in keeping,
Since I must go, now day is near.'

ANONYMOUS
seventeenth century

We kissed at the barrier; and passing
   through
She left me, and moment by
   moment got
Smaller and smaller, until to my view
  She was but a spot:

A wee white spot of muslin fluff
That down the diminishing platform
   bore
Through hustling crowds of gentle
   and rough
  To the carriage door.

THOMAS HARDY,
poet and novelist, 1840–1928

When we two parted
In silence and tears,
Half broken-hearted
To sever for years,
Pale grew thy cheek and cold,
Colder thy kiss;
Truly that hour foretold
Sorrow to this.

LORD GEORGE BYRON,
poet, 1788–1824

What of the soul was left, I wonder, when the kissing had to stop?

ROBERT BROWNING,
poet, 1812–89

'Once and no more,' so said my love
  When in mine arms enchained.
She unto mine her lips did move,
  And so my heart had gained.
This done, she said, 'Away I must
  For fear of being missed.
Your heart's made over but in trust.'
  And so again she kissed.

ANONYMOUS,
seventeenth century

Ae fond kiss, and then we sever,
  Ae fareweel, and then for ever!
Deep in heart-wrung tears I'll pledge
    thee!
  Warring sighs and groans I'll wage
    thee! ...
Had we never lov'd sae kindly –
  Had we never lov'd sae blindly –
Never met – or never parted,
  We had ne'er been broken-hearted.

ROBERT BURNS,
poet, 1759–96

Acknowledgements

There are copyrights I could not trace. The publishers will be happy to rectify any omissions in future editions. I would like to thank the following:

Pam Brown, Pamela Dugdale and Barry Keen (London's gentlest dentist) for permission to quote their thoughts on kissing.

Curtis Brown: reproduced with permission of Curtis Brown Group Ltd, London, on behalf of Eric Robinson. Copyright © Eric Robinson 1966.

Duke University Press for an extract from *The Collected Letters of Thomas and Jane Welsh Carlyle*, edited by Charles Richard Sanders *et al.*, Duke University Press, Durham, North Carolina, 1970, vol. 4.

Eric Glass: for an extract from *Alban Berg: Letter to his Wife*, edited, translated and annotated by Bernard Grun, published by Faber and Faber, by permission of Eric Glass Ltd.

The Random House Group for permission for and extract from *The Young Visiters* by Daisy Ashford, published by Chatto & Windus. Reprinted by permission of The Random House Group Ltd.

Random House, Inc. New York, for permission to quote from *Love Signals* by David B. Givens, copyright © 1983. Used by permission of Crown Publishers, a division of Random House, Inc.

The Society of Authors as the Literary Representative of the Estate of Richard Le Gallienne for permission for an extract from the *Quest of The Golden Girl* by Richard Le Gallienne.